A Decade of
FRENCH FASHION
1929–1938: FROM THE DEPRESSION TO THE BRINK OF WAR

MARY CAROLYN WALDREP

DOVER PUBLICATIONS, INC.
MINEOLA, NEW YORK

Bibliographical Note

A Decade of French Fashion, 1929-1938: From the Depression to the Brink of War, first published by Dover Publications, Inc., in 2015, is a new selection of illustrations from the following sources: *Les grands modeles,* Journal Periodique, Paris, 1929; *Modeles originaux beaux-arts des modes,* Chic Parisien, Paris, December 1932; *Chic parisien publication mensuelle,* Chic Parisien , Paris, January, June, July, August, 1933; *Modeles originaux beaux-arts des modes,* Chic Parisien, Paris, ca. 1935/36, August 1938.

International Standard Book Number

ISBN-13: 978-0-486-79783-0
ISBN-10: 0-486-79783-X

Manufactured in the United States by Courier Corporation
79783X01   2015
www.doverpublications.com

Beginning in the 1890s and continuing into the middle of the 20th century, publishers such as Journal Périodique and Chic Parisien produced books of fashion plates for the international market. Complete with back views, notes on fashion trends, and captions detailing fabrics and styling details in French, English, and German, these books showcased the latest in French fashion. These books were published monthly or bimonthly with twice-yearly supplements. The books were sold in the United States by a variety of distributors. The eight volumes featured here were distributed by three different New York companies — S. Reinach Company in 1929, Haire Fashion Publications in 1932 and 1933, and Imported Fashion Books, Inc. in 1938. The eighth publication had no cover, although it appears to be from 1935/1936.

These beautiful full color plates offer firsthand evidence of the dramatic change in fashion in the period between the world wars.

In the aftermath of the "Great War," both men and women embraced new freedom in lifestyle and fashion as traditional roles and mores began to change. For women, the trend to a more relaxed silhouette, which had started before the war, became even more pronounced. By the middle of the 1920s, fashionable skirts were at the knee and a slim, boyish silhouette was all the rage. This silhouette, although quite narrow at the top, exploded with movement from the hips down — pleats, ruffles, and godets gave ease to skirts, allowing women to stride forth with confidence. Skirts began to drop slightly by the end of the decade, often by means of uneven hems, but in general, the silhouette remained in fashion through the end of the decade. Although the style was by no means adapted by everyone, the prevailing image of the 1920s woman is the flapper with short skirts and bobbed hair.

The free and easy Jazz Age came to a halt in late October 1929 when stock prices began to fall precipitously, culminating on October 29, enshrined in American folklore as Black Tuesday. Stocks continued to decline over the next few weeks, recovered briefly, but then the country slid inexorably into the Great Depression. By 1933 more than 20% of America's population was unemployed, and many of those who still had jobs had taken a pay cut.

Fashion, too, took an abrupt turn as women turned to a more conservative, ladylike look. Hemlines plummeted, the waistline moved to a more natural position, and shoulders widened. For many, "make do" was the fashion watchword of the decade. Clothes were patched and remade and, when absolutely necessary, replaced with the inexpensive ready-to-wear from outlets such as Sears, Roebuck, and Co. and Montgomery Ward. Nevertheless, fashion is hard to suppress, and America's women craved glamour as represented by the stars they saw on the silver screen. Indeed, the burgeoning film industry soon became even more influential on style than the Paris fashion houses.

The prevailing look of the thirties was long and lean, with hemlines reaching the bottom of the calf by 1932, and then beginning a slow rise to just below the knee by the end of the decade. The silhouette was very fluid, with draping and bias cutting emphasizing the body. Skirts were very narrow, with slim godets, pleats, or gathers providing walking ease. Bodices were draped, asymmetrical, crossed, wrapped, peplumed, and trimmed with openwork, ruffles, pleats, and bow collars, while sleeves came in infinite variety — leg of mutton, puffed, raglan, kimono, and more. Novelty seaming, both curved and angular, was seen on both skirts and bodices. The full-skirted tunic top over a slim skirt for both day and evening became popular, and after a decade of being ignored, the waistline was emphasized with belts, sashes, and insets. Jackets, ranging in length from bolero to hip-length, became a fashion staple, worn over dresses as well as skirts and blouses, and fur — lamb, fox, mink, or rabbit — became the trim of choice, banding sleeves, hems and necklines.

By 1938, styles were beginning to be more severe and less fluid, with shorter skirts and less draping, foreshadowing the pared-down styles of the World War II years.

Smart ensemble of soft crayon green wool. Both dress and coat have inserted godets.
White crêpe de chine plastron with a stylish bow. The collar and cuffs of the coat
are made of sealskin.

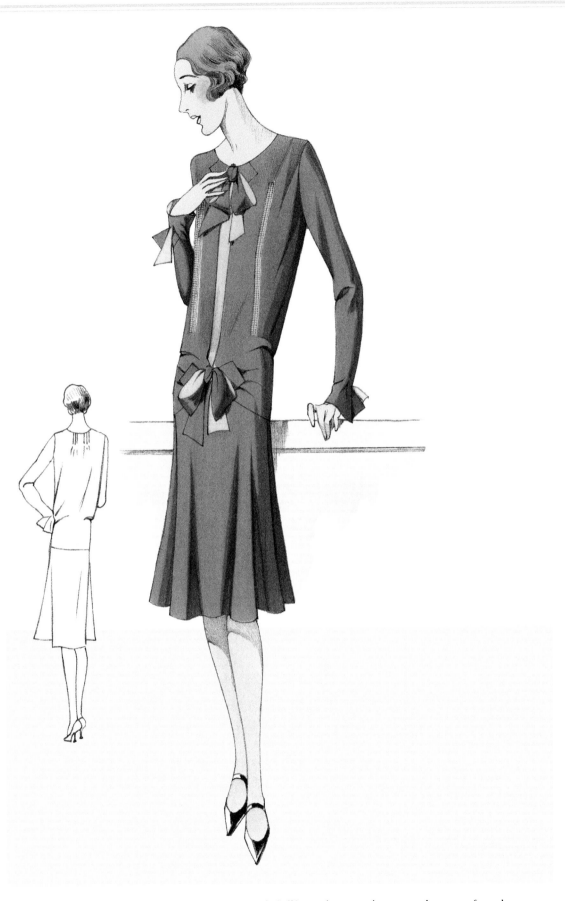

Smart afternoon frock of blue crêpe mongol (silk), with vertical openwork over a foundation
of absinthe crêpe mongol. The bows are lined with absinthe.

Smart frock of pepita (checked) wool. Simple belted style, with pointed godets.
Plastron of white crêpe georgette, brown cravat.

Afternoon frock of pink crêpe de chine, with novelty "apron."
Trimmed with buttons and a belt buckle of dull gold.

Afternoon dress of emerald green crêpe satin with rows of curved seams.
The back view shows dipping godets. In front a self-fabric bow, lined with white crêpe satin.

Evening dress of panné velvet in a soft crayon blue.
Graduated pleats of varying length form the shaped skirt.

Frock of crayon blue wool crêpe. Small belt of self-fabric. Unusual seams continue as godets.
Neck-band and cuffs of beige wool crêpe with button trim.

Fascinating ensemble of gray wool. Coat built on straight lines with a shawl cut in one with the body. Trimming of fur to match. Frock of wool crêpe with pleats on each side of the skirt. Slot pockets outlined with stitching and novelty seams form the trimming.

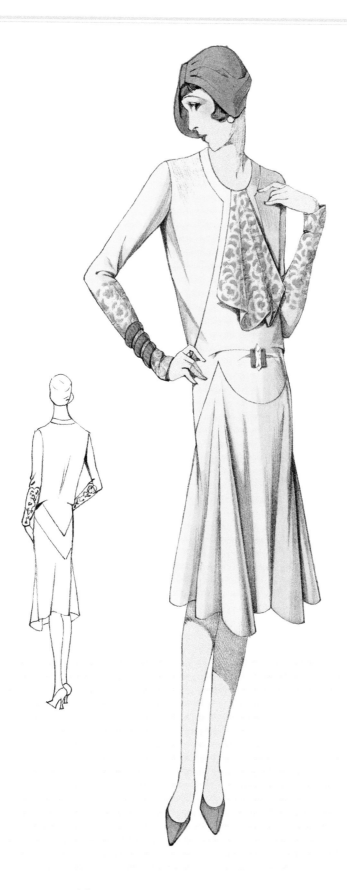

Afternoon frock of absinthe crêpe mongol (silk), with unusual seaming.
The skirt falls into elongated godets. Jabot and bottom of the sleeves
are entirely adorned with embroidery.

Smart frock of fine wool in a soft pastel shade. The interesting skirt forms box pleats that dip gracefully. Neck and sleeves adorned with French crêpe.

Afternoon frock of dull green patterned crêpe satin. One-sided style with tiers forming godets,
dipping on the right and caught up on the left, showing a foundation of self-fabric.
The neck is finished with a large bow.

Smart afternoon frock of brown crêpe mongol (silk). Asymmetrical style with irregular godets dipping on the right. Neck and revers of silk lace in same color. Belt finished with a buckle of dull gold.

Stylish afternoon frock of crayon blue crêpe mongol (silk), richly trimmed with point-lace
made of self-fabric. This model forms a fan of godets on the right and is finished with a bow on the left.
Sleeves with smart musketeer cuffs.

Elegant frock of wool crêpe. Stitching at the top of the pleated skirt simulates a yoke.
The top is trimmed with asymmetrical bands of self-fabric and finished with a pleated band.

Modish princess frock in bolero style, made of beige wool crêpe. The bolero, the hip bands, and the cravat of self-fabric are finished with a narrow edging. The skirt shows soft godets in a graceful line.

Street frock of pepita (checked) wool, built on simple lines and showing loose godets.
Lapels, plastron, and trimming of plain wool.

Dinner frock of blue taffeta in a juvenile style. Skirt with irregular flounces, forming capricious pleats. Big shoulder flowers of self-fabric.

Dress of soft wool in light crayon red. One-sided style; bloused top slightly draped and continued as a yoke. Musketeer cuffs, metal ball buttons.

Afternoon frock of fine blue wool crêpe, simulating a bolero, which is buttoned onto a lime-green crêpe mongol (silk) plastron. The skirt features flared panels of self-fabric.

Evening frock of emerald green crêpe georgette or silk muslin. The bolero has an oval neckline and
is continued as a long train. The foundation skirt forms loose pleats on the side.

Ball gown of brocade lamé. Low-placed belt of brocade and velvet,
looped trimming, gold lamé shoulder straps.
Chiffon velvet cape, long velvet gloves.

A. Informal evening gown of velvet. High front neck, interesting back décolletage. Fur-trimmed cape sleeves and skirt hem.

B. Sleeveless jacket banded with fur and fastened with a rhinestone buckle.

Evening dress of chiffon velvet. Interesting back décolletage, skirt slashed on the left side and faced in contrasting color. Short wrap of shirred dark chiffon velvet with mink banding.

A. Informal evening dress of georgette
   and Venetian lace. Shoulder yoke
   with floating crossed ends.
B. Velvet coat. Collar and sleeves
   trimmed with seal.

A

B

Empire style ball gown of chiffon velvet; gauze foliage in a lighter shade surround the armholes.

White satin evening robe. Shoulder strap and belt embroidered with rhinestones.
Corsage in one with scarf, mink or fox banding. Roll collar and scarf faced with silk velvet.

A. Evening robe of satin. Deep V-neck and armholes trimmed with rhinestone galloon.
   Ascending front, slender sides. Contrasting color velvet gloves with cuffs.
B. Hip length velvet jacket with mink collar and banding.

A. Afternoon dress of brocaded silk crêpe.
and Irish lace.
B. Velvet coat with a big beaver collar and border.

A. Day dress of wool. Asymmetrical collar banded with baby lamb laid around the right arm.
   Epaulet of lamb on the left. Skirt has asymmetrical seaming.
B. Crossed capelet, tie collar and muff of baby lamb.

A. Afternoon dress in velvet. Sleeves
are fitted to mid bicep, puffed below.
Collar and cuffs of Irish lace,
passementerie belt.

B. Seal bolero with high crossed fastening.

A. Dress of patterned angora knit. Slot seams are underlaid with colored knit. Raglan sleeves, striped
    knit scarf, leather belt and gauntlets. Hip yoke is cut in one with skirt front and back.

B. Coat of matching, but coarser material, repeating the effects of the dress.

A. Afternoon dress. Six gore velvet skirt, lamé tunic, bow finished with passementerie tassel. Crossed fronts, cut with slender belt.

B. Velvet jacket banded with Persian lamb.

A. Afternoon dress of crêpe Bamboula.
   Yoke and leg of mutton sleeves
   worked on net. Yoked skirt with
   a godet in the front.
B. Crossed nutria bolero.

A. Dress of marocain (ribbed farbric).
   Shoulder yoke with passementerie bow.
   Interesting décolletage and sleeves.
   Plain skirt with a godet on the left.
B. Broadcloth coat trimmed in the same way.
   Collar of Persian lamb.

A. Afternoon dress of marocain (ribbed
   fabric) has a long princess peplum
   with inverted pleats and leg of mutton
   sleeves. Crêpe de chine collar and cuffs.
B. Broadcloth coat with a big collar
   banded with seal.

Error

1932 ∾ 35

A. Afternoon dress in two colors of velvet; kimono bodice,
   skirt with inlaid hip piece.
B. Hip length jacket trimmed with Persian lamb.

A. Afternoon dress of artificial silk crêpe. Skirt with draped sides creating a
   tunic effect. Two shades of crêpe de chine serves as the trimming.
B. Cloth coat with seal collar and sleeves.

A

B

A. Afternoon dress of wool lace with
   shaded georgette trim. Low-placed
   double belt, metal buckle. Raglan
   sleeves with self-fabric loops.
B. Velvet coat with mink or ermine
   collar and high gauntlets.

A. Afternoon suit in velvet, hip length jacket with wide shoulders, curved fronts, and seal shawl collar
   and banding. The skirt features two godets in the front.
B. Blouse of lighter shaded silk crêpe with low shoulder yoke.

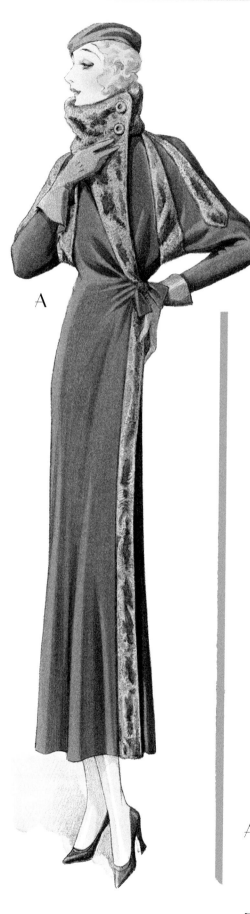

A

B

A. Handsome coat of kashamoussa (wool flannel) trimmed with baby lamb. Plastron collar closed on side with fur buttons. Kimono sleeves, tied in the front.

B. Dress of dull and shiny satin made in the same way.

A. Afternoon dress of marocain (ribbed fabric) with pale marocain trim and hand-sewn openwork.

B–C. Cape of baby lamb.

D. Silk crêpe frock with braid embroidery on the georgette collar, tie ,and cuffs. Leg-of-mutton sleeves.

E. Broadcloth or velvet coat with beaver collar.

F. Afternoon dress of crêpe, crossed bodice, leg-of-mutton sleeves, pale georgette collar and cuffs.

G–H. Velvet bolero collar and cuffs edged with fur.

A. Afternoon dress of panné velvet, shawl shaped top, slim collar and sleeve trim of plain silk velvet. Skirt is draped at the left.

B. Flamisol (fine silk fabric with a dull, finely grained surface) frock with interesting raglan sleeves. Belt of chenille cords with tassels.

C. Afternoon dress of patterned crêpe. Slashed raglan sleeves, self-fabric belt drawn through metal loops, four-gore skirt.

A. Evening dress of sheer velvet. Pointed bodice, skirt with slender godet sides and inset scallops.
Sequin embroidered shoulder ribbons crossed behind. Scarf of gathered silk jersey.
B. Evening dress of croquignol. Arm bands and belt of lamé, embroidered with stones. Flaring basque,
skirt draped in front.

A. Street frock in black wool, shoulders widened by pleats, white piqué trim, patent leather belt, pockets trimmed like the cuffs.

B. Street frock of plain knit fabric with plaid knit trim. Yoke with joined epaulets, tie drawn through an opening in the yoke, leather belt. Plaid gloves.

A. Afternoon dress of marocain (ribbed fabric), plastron, lower part of sleeve, and belt of plain
   marocain with metal and wood beads. Puffed sleeves. Collar of marocain and gold lamé strips.
B. Dress of silk crêpe with silver tissue trim and colored enamel buckles. Dress has raglan sleeves,
   underlaid cuffs and inserted godets in the front and back.
C. Dress of chiffon velvet. Top in satin with silver stripes. High-waisted skirt. Hip-length jacket with
   raglan sleeves and skunk band.

A. Dress of coarsely ribbed wool with differently cut sections. Three-colored baby lamb tie and
   gauntlet-gloves. Metal buttons.

B. Street frock of diagonal wool, with decorative buttons, leather belt, and cross grain pockets.
   Broadtail cape and muff pocket effects.

C. Dress of jersey or wool velvet trimmed with jersey in three tones. Wide armholes, joined skirt with
   broad folds.

A. Promenade dress of printed foulard. Fagoted plastron and fitted sleeves of georgette, draped collar and ample oversleeves with ruffles.

B. Afternoon dress of plain and printed mongol (silk). Draped collar tied on the side, elbow length puff sleeves.

C. Afternoon dress of marocain (ribbed fabric). Openwork detail on bodice, slashed sleeves cut in one with the body, skirt divided behind, satin belt tied in a bow at the back.

A. Summer suit. Short jacket of diagonally striped wool, plain wool straight skirt. Shawl collar; tie-belt of plain wool.

B. Jersey suit. Hip-length jacket, applied waistcoat of white piqué. Patent leather belt; patch pockets, godet skirt.

C. Promenade costume. Two-button jacket of light polished satin, skirt of dark polished satin. Pocket flaps, clusters of pleats at lower front of skirt.

A. Racecourse dress of georgette. Open-stitched bows and sleeve sections of lace. Slightly draped top, pointed godets on skirt.

B. Derby dress of lace. Divided collar with epaulet sections. Satin sash belt tied in a big bow in front. Neckpiece of fox skins.

C. Promenade ensemble. Frock of printed georgette. Curved bands on the skirt and sleeves. Three-quarter length full coat with flounced sleeves and rabbit border.

A. Evening gown of pale and dark lace. The dress top simulates a jacket; the sleeves are cut in one with the body. Skirt with godets comes to a point at the center front of the high waist.

B. Juvenile evening dress of georgette. Dress has shoulder straps, flounced white sleevelets, diagonally ascending skirt flounces, and a velvet belt.

C. Evening ensemble of satin. Sleevelets and short evening jacket are striped diagonally, the jacket has frilled sleeves cut in one with the body, a shawl collar, and a tie belt.

A. Afternoon dress of wool crêpe. Bloused bodice with fagoting and open sleeves. Plastron and tie in georgette, belt and decorative motifs of satin.

B. Printed crêpe de chine frock with crossed bodice, balloon sleeves, and an organza ruffled collar. Wool crêpe three-quarter length coat with openwork trim.

C. Afternoon dress of printed mongol (silk). Collar, plastron, and sleeve bands of organza; inverted fold in front.

A. Golf ensemble. Yoked tweed skirt with pockets, two box pleats in front, one at the back. Blouse and
   scarf of checked cotton. Three-quarter length flannel coat.
B. Tennis outfit. Divided skirt of white flannel, jersey blouse with embroidered emblems, crêpe de chine
   scarf. Blue flannel jacket.
C. Sports ensemble. Princess dress in white cotton panama (plain-weave summer suiting) with double
   pockets, laced plastron, and inverted pleats. Coat of pale wool.

A. Traveling ensemble. Skirt and cape of wool tweed, cape lining and scarf of striped jersey. Inserted pockets.

B. Traveling suit of jersey. Short, loose jacket with clips. Plaid jersey tie. Inverted pleats on skirt folds.

C. Travelling ensemble. Plaid djalap (thin, hairy-surfaced fabric) or angora skirt, loose seven-eights-length coat of coarse wool, plaid silk scarf.

A. Summer frock in printed mongol (silk). Pleated windmill bow, asymmetrical collar and tie of white
 piqué or georgette, open sleeves with pleats. Pleated skirt front.

B. Afternoon dress of silk crêpe in two shades with openwork detail. Removable capelet.

A. Informal evening dress of plaid organza. Wide armholes, interesting back décolletage, sash.

B. Evening dress of white satin with colored georgette trim. Wide bows cut in one with the back, belt of two georgette bands. Skirt extends into a slight train. Georgette gloves.

C. Evening dress of embroidered organza. Shirred ruching at neck, wing sleeves, satin belt and flower.

A. Racecourse dress of printed silk voile with pleated flounces. Hip length jacket with open, short sleeves. Fabric flower trim.

B. Princess robe in georgette, curved, pleated self-ruffles, georgette collar and tie, puffed short sleeves.

C. Mongol (silk) dress with removable capelet edged with looped trim. Collar, tie, and sleeves of organza.

D. Racecourse ensemble in printed silk gauze, shaped flounces, bodice forms a type of a fichu.

E. Racecourse ensemble in striped foulard. Openwork top in georgette with georgette and deerskin belt.

F. Dress of marocain (ribbed fabric). Asymmetrical décolletage, bow and edging of organza, half sleeves with small puffs, fan pleats on skirt.

G. Racecourse ensemble of printed chiffon trimmed with fagoting. Open sleeves, satin belt, clips and flowers in matching tones.

H. Racecourse ensemble of printed chiffon. Princess dress with short sleeves, tie with chiffon flowers. Full coat of plain chiffon trimmed with fox.

A. Afternoon dress of marocain (ribbed fabric) and contrasting crêpe de chine, trimmed with bias seams. Sleeves feature loop-shaped cutouts on a colored underlay.

B. Afternoon dress of crêpe de chine with yoke and sleeve trim of tucked organza, wool embroidery, twisted velvet ribbon.

C. Afternoon dress of printed mongol (silk), open sleeves with bows, matching bows on neck and belt. Inverted pleats.

A. Racecourse dress of white organza. Flounces serve as trimming and sleeves, belt of wide
satin ribbon.

B. Racecourse ensemble. Princess dress in printed chiffon, with horizontally tucked front, big muslin
bow, and draped skirt. Three-quarter-length marocain (ribbed fabric) coat with rabbit fur band.

A. Summer frock in striped washable silk. Blouse with yoke and shoulder band, white piqué trim, and patent leather belt. Box-pleated skirt. Short full coat of wool crêpe.
B. Skirt and capelet of wool crêpe, patterned silk blouse with bolero effect. Capelet has pleated shoulders. Skirt has inset panels.

A. Silk gauze frock for a garden party. Peplum blouse with self-fabric belt. Cape edged with ruching. Skirt with draped godets.

B. Dress for garden-party of printed organza with pleated ruffles. Shoulder straps and belt of two-colored georgette.

A. Wool crêpe frock trimmed with plaid wool crêpe, tie and sleeve bands of piqué, inserted pleats.

B. Ensemble of natural linen, tie and bows of striped foulard, novelty pockets, accordion pleats on skirt. Jacket with pleated epaulets.

C. Shantung silk frock; sleeves, yoke, and tab of white shantung. Slot pockets.

A. Afternoon dress of flamisol (fine silk fabric with a dull, finely grained surface) and plaid crêpe de chine. Radiating tucks at the shoulders, self-fabric belt, skirt with hip yoke and tucked draping on the left.

B. Summer frock in printed China crêpe, short sleeves with raglan effect, collar and belt of satin, removable capelet with clusters of pleats.

C. Ensemble of horizontally-striped satin and plain wool crêpe. Slashed bodice edged with cross-grain bands; white georgette plastron; skirt with inverted pleats. Three-quarter length straight cut coat with scarf collar.

A. Morning dress of diagonally-
striped wool with stitched
trimming. Top simulates a bolero.
Tie and sleeve of caracul.

B. Swagger coat in plain wool with
caracul collar and sleeve band.

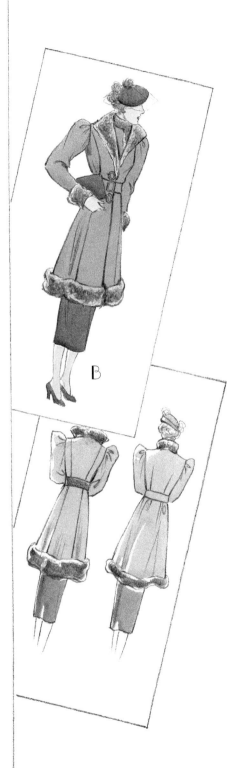

A. Afternoon ensemble. Tunic of dark green velvet, banded with astrakhan. Sleeves puffed at the shoulders. Dark crêpe skirt.

B. Velvet coat styled like the tunic.

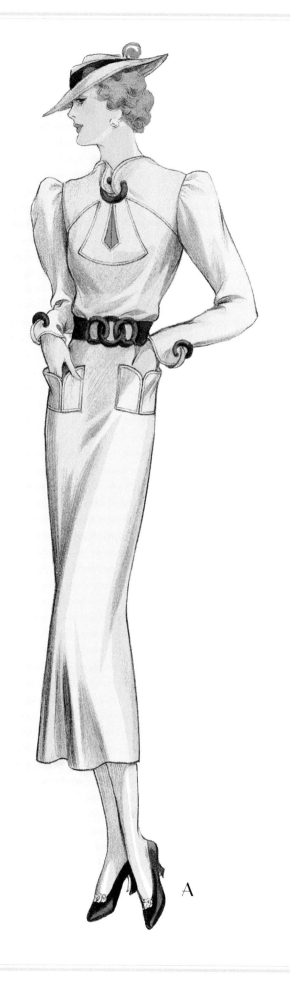

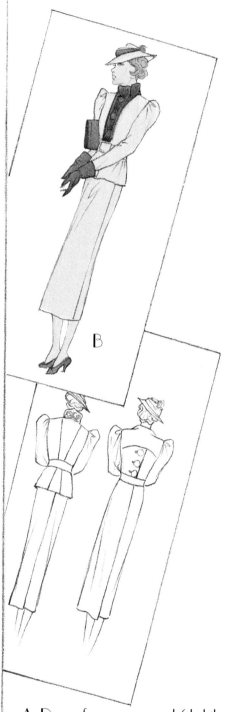

A. Dress of crêpe jarré wool (slightly coarse wool). Sleeves are puffed at the shoulders. Belt and loops at neck at cuffs of leather, patch pockets, series of large buttons on the back.

B. Crêpe jarré wool jacket. Fur collar and front band.

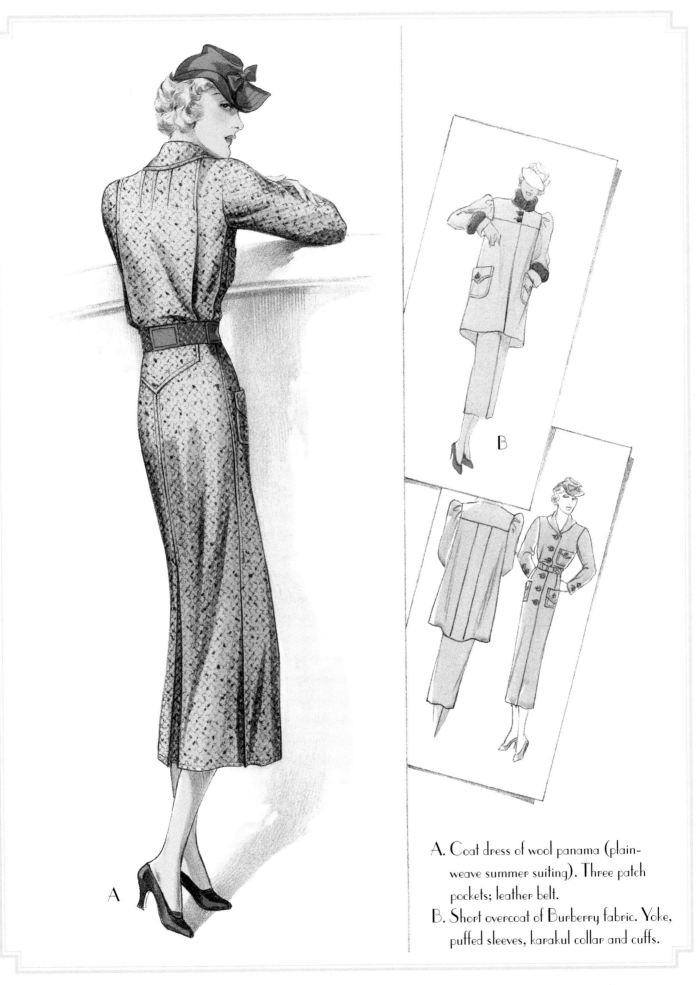

A. Coat dress of wool panama (plain-weave summer suiting). Three patch pockets; leather belt.

B. Short overcoat of Burberry fabric. Yoke, puffed sleeves, karakul collar and cuffs.

A. Afternoon ensemble. Tunic of plain
   wool crêpe; sleeve and lower edge
   trimmed with padded and stitched
   circles, open sleeves, rhinestone clip,
   satin sash. Wool crêpe skirt.
B. Long jacket of wool crêpe and caracul.

A. Afternoon dress of medium blue wool. Loose hanging sleeves with wide openings lined in lighter blue. Draped collar open over a bi-color plastron. Slim skirt with soft pleats on the front panel.

B. Wool coat with lynx collar and trim.

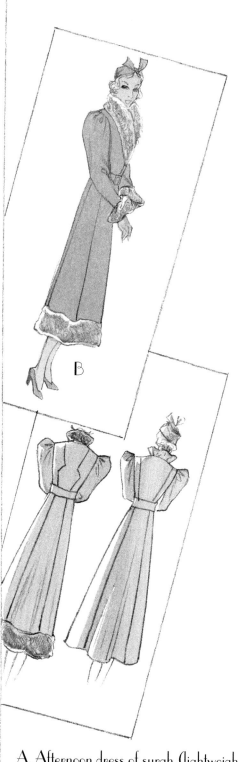

A. Afternoon dress of surah (lightweight twill silk). Ruffled collar and sleeve bands edged with pleated white organza, leg-of-mutton sleeves, buttoned band down front edge of skirt.

B. Duvella (type of wool) coat, leg-of-mutton sleeves. Collar, cuffs, and lower edge banded with caracul.

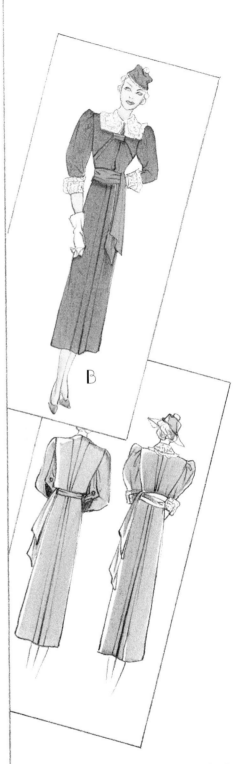

A. Bolero of wool crêpe. Collar, high
   cuffs, and muff of caracul.
B. Wool crêpe dress. Lace collar and cuffs,
   bias seams on bodice, contrasting color
   knotted silk belt tied at the side.

A. Afternoon ensemble. Full-skirted satin
   tunic with puffed raglan sleeves. Two
   wide stitched-down pleats at the center
   front form a "breastplate." Self-fabric
   scarf belt, wool straight skirt.
B. Long wool jacket wool edged with fox.

A. Afternoon dress in matte and shiny satin, narrow shawl collar, puffed raglan sleeves with diamond-shaped openwork.

B. Coat of soft wook trimmed with mink.

A. Afternoon dress of pabrilla. Delicately
    embroidered bib and cuffs of white pabrilla.
B. Wool coat with caracul collar and facings.

A. Matte crêpe business dress. Top inlaid
with strips of gauze on a contrasting
color base. Velvet ribbon tie, galalith
(early type of plastic) belt buckle.
Tunic-like apron.

B. Coat trimmed with strips of Persian
lamb, puffed sleeves.

A. Moiré silk cocktail dress with
    basque bodice. Deep neckline at
    the back; back peplum gathered
    below the waist; velvet collar,
    waistband and cuffs. Elbow
    length puffed sleeves.
B. Velvet coat trimmed with fox.

A. Afternoon ensemble of satin. Full-skirted tunic over a straight skirt, mesh openwork at neck and on the short puffed sleeves.

B. Coat of brocaded silk with leg-of-mutton sleeves; collar and lower edge banded with mink.

A. Georgette evening dress trimmed with applied taffeta ribbons, cap sleeves, long full cut skirt.

B. Long wool cape with a velvet yoke.

A. Sleeveless satin evening gown with a deep V neckline over a small tulle fichu. Skirt split at front, arm openings and lower edge trimmed with tulle ruffles, rhinestone buttons.

B. Ruffled tulle cape.

A. Evening gown of changeable
   taffeta. Basque bodice with short
   puffed sleeves, gored skirt. Sleeves,
   bodice front, and lower edge of skirt
   are trimmed with small flowers of
   self-fabric.
B. Ermine cape with peplum.

A. Evening gown. Sleeveless tunic of
   silver lamé, shoulder straps fixed by
   rhinestone buttons at the back, lower
   edge banded with silver fox. Narrow
   satin skirt split at center front.
B. Velvet coat with fox collar and cuffs.

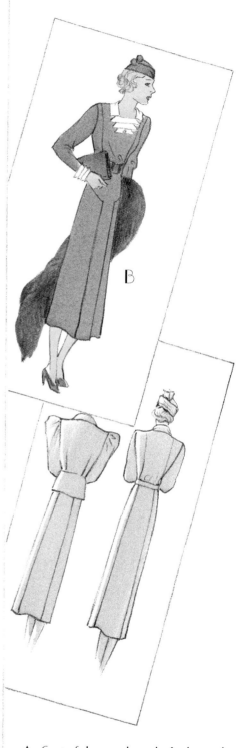

A. Suit of diagonal wool. Jacket with leg-of-mutton sleeves, a wide collar, and curved lower edges. Narrow skirt with stitched-down pleats.

B. Matching blouse of silk crêpe with novelty collar and cuffs of white silk.

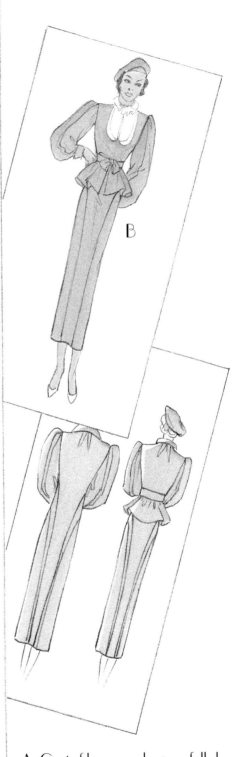

A. Coat of heavy wool crêpe , full sleeves,
   shawl collar, second collar of fur.

B. Dress of mongol (silk). Fitted basque
   bodice with white bib, and gathered
   peplum.

A. Wool suit. Princess line, hip-length jacket with curved lower edge, fur collar. Straight skirt.

B. Satin blouse with soft tie collar and self belt.

A. Silk crêpe blouse with short peplum, extended shoulders, low puffed sleeves, draped collar.

B. Silk blouse with buttoned yoke, round collar, pockets, three-quarter length sleeves, and banded waist

C. Full-skirted satin crêpe tunic; contrasting collar, belt, and bodice bands.

D. Blouse of dark brown mongol (silk). Round yoke, full sleeves. Pink taffeta forms the draped collar, lines the self belt, and trims the cuffs.

E. Silk blouse; raglan sleeves; pleated jabot, basque and cuffs.

Dress of colored wool. Skirt joined at the waistline, buttoned at the side;
cross-over bodice buttoned at the opposite side. Edged with broad satin ribbon.

Afternoon dress of crêpe in two shades. Yoke trimmed with a row of tiny buttons. Full bloused bodice, drawn-through sash, and flat collar of contrasting color.

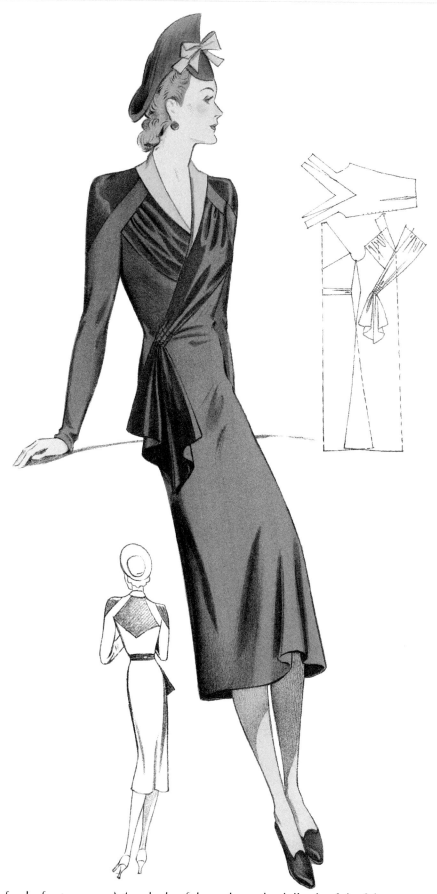

Afternoon frock of satin crêpe. Main body of dress shows the dull side of the fabric; cross-over front, top of sleeves, and sash show the shiny side. Collar of pastel georgette.

Two-piece brown marocain (ribbed fabric) frock with vertical tucks and
gold braid with georgette piping.

Afternoon frock of mongol (silk). The jabot section which is cut in one with the bodice falls in waves.
Front panel of skirt ascends to a point and is slightly shirred at the top waistline.

Afternoon frock. Back fastening. Cross-over front with one-sided revers overlaid with pastel crêpe du chine.
Back and front shirred along midriff, embroidered motif at revers and hip.

Two-piece frock of fine jersey with rich diagonal tucked trimming. Flat collar.
Sweater buttons all the way down. Slightly flared skirt.

Afternoon frock of cloqué (silk, rayon, or cotton
fabric with a raised woven pattern) with back
fastening. Top is draped from bands of
grosgrain ribbon. Bow at the side.

Frock of pale wool crêpe with belt and shawl in darker shade. There is a row of embroidery
down the front and sleeves. Soft tie at neck.

Afternoon frock of cloqué, (silk, rayon, or
cotton fabric with a raised woven pattern)
draped asymmetrically, with revers falling
in soft folds over a lamé plastron.

Wool dress with bolero-shaped, slightly bloused bodice and vestee of stitched silk.

Afternoon frock of marocain (ribbed fabric) with interesting applied flower trim.
Vestee of georgette with stem-shaped appliqués.

Afternoon frock of wool with wide horizontal insert of pink lamé continuing at the sleeves.
The top forms cornets, which are doubled with lamé.

Asymmetrically draped afternoon frock of wool with bands and bows in contrasting color at the top and on the sleeves. Skirt has off-center folds, held by smocking at the waistline.

Princess line evening frock of white faille. Shirred bands of pastel georgette at the hemline,
rosettes of the same fabric at the shoulders.

Theater frock with white taffeta bodice. High-waisted skirt joined in scallops of black lace.
Black lace inserts at the sleeves.

Evening gown of wool with low V back, draped high to the neck in front.
Skirt joined at the waistline, fullness begins at the triangular smock motifs.

Evening gown of lamé with back, sash, and shawl sections of chiffon velvet.

Evening gown of matte crêpe and chiffon in two pastel shades.
Corselet skirt of crêpe, bodice with loose panels of chiffon.

Late afternoon frock of matte crêpe. Bloused bodice
pleated like the skirt front. Buttoned hip-yoke.

Suit of wool satin. Jacket with rounded basques; hemline and plastron ection tucked.
Narrow vestee and collar of seal.

Draped wool bouclé winter coat with surplice closing.
Vertical inserts at back; shawl sections of seal or nutria.

Late afternoon frock of Bourdelyon, slightly shirred below the small yoke.
Sash and inserted front panel of the skirt of chiffon in a contrasting hue.